MY FAVORITE DOG

YORKSHIRE TERRIERS

by Anna Davison, MS
Dog Expert: Beth Adelman, MS
Former editor, *American Kennel Club Gazette*

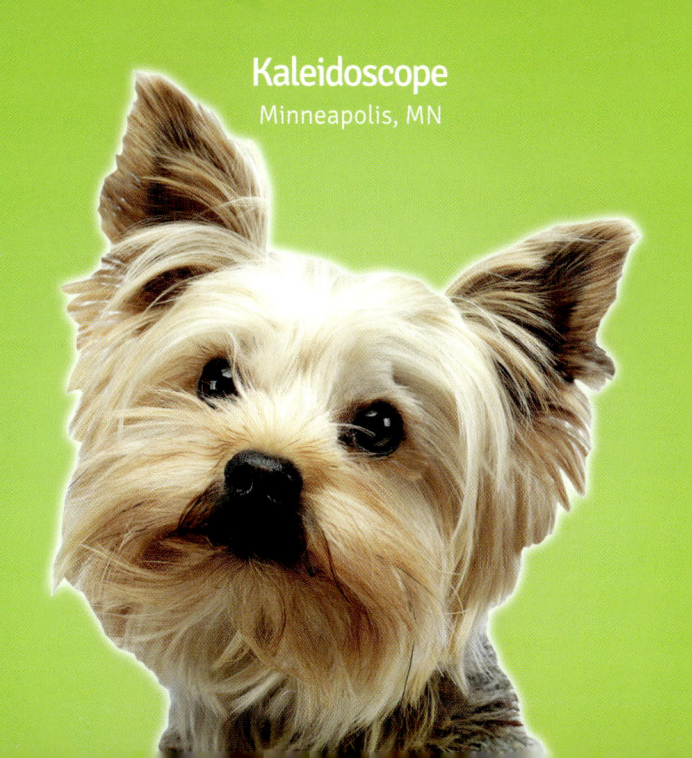

Kaleidoscope
Minneapolis, MN

Bigfoot Books

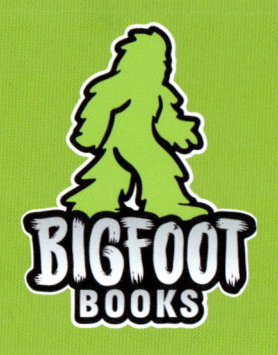

The Quest for Discovery Never Ends

This edition first published in 2021 by Kaleidoscope Publishing, Inc.

No part of this publication may be reproduced in whole or in part without written permission of the publisher.

For information regarding permission, write to
Kaleidoscope Publishing, Inc.
6012 Blue Circle Drive
Minnetonka, MN 55343

Library of Congress Control Number
2020936243

ISBN
978-1-64519-447-7 (library bound)
978-1-64519-459-0 (ebook)

Text copyright © 2021 by Kaleidoscope Publishing, Inc. All-Star Sports, Bigfoot Books, and associated logos are trademarks and/or registered trademarks of Kaleidoscope Publishing, Inc.

Printed in the United States of America.

FIND ME IF YOU CAN!

Bigfoot lurks within one of the images in this book. It's up to you to find him!

TABLE OF
CONTENTS

Introduction 4

Chapter 1: The Story of Yorkshire Terriers 6

Chapter 2: Looking at a Yorkie 12

Chapter 3: Meet a Yorkshire Terrier! 16

Chapter 4: Caring for a Yorkie 22

Beyond the Book 28
Research Ninja 29
Further Resources 30
Glossary 31
Index 32
Photo Credits 32
About the Author 32

Introduction
Here Comes a Yorkie!

When Sophie took her dog, Yoyo, out into the yard for the first time, she heard a voice. "Is that real?" asked her neighbor, peeping over the fence. Sophie looked at her new four-legged friend. Yoyo was tiny. He had a little black button nose and long, flowing hair. He was so small and so cute that he did almost look like a stuffed animal!

FUN FACT
The American Kennel Club lists 29 breeds of dog with "Terrier" in their name.

5

Chapter 1
The Story of Yorkshire Terriers

Yoyo is a Yorkshire Terrier, or a Yorkie for short. These dogs come from Yorkshire, an area in the north of Great Britain. They were originally bred to be hunters. Yorkies worked in cloth factories and mines. They chased after pesky mice and rats. They were small and determined.

Yorkshire Terriers were first brought to the United States in the 1870s. But by the 1880s, most of these dogs didn't have jobs. By then, most Yorkies were family pets. They were just so cute that people wanted one on their lap!

Now, the Yorkshire Terrier is one of the most popular breeds in the United States.

FUN FACT

The first Yorkies were bred from three different terriers brought from Scotland to England.

Yorkshire Terriers come in black, tan, gold, and silvery-blue. They are usually a combination of a couple of colors. The hair on Yoyo's back is black and silver, but his legs and face are golden brown.

Yoyo has ears like little triangles. They stick up from the top of his head. When he smells something interesting, his little black nose wiggles. He has dark eyes that sparkle.

When he walks, Yoyo's short tail sticks up and he holds his head high. He looks like he's proud to be a Yorkie!

FAMOUS YORKIE

A Yorkie named Smoky helped out during World War II. She also worked as a therapy dog, visiting soldiers who had been hurt. After the war, Smoky became a TV star!

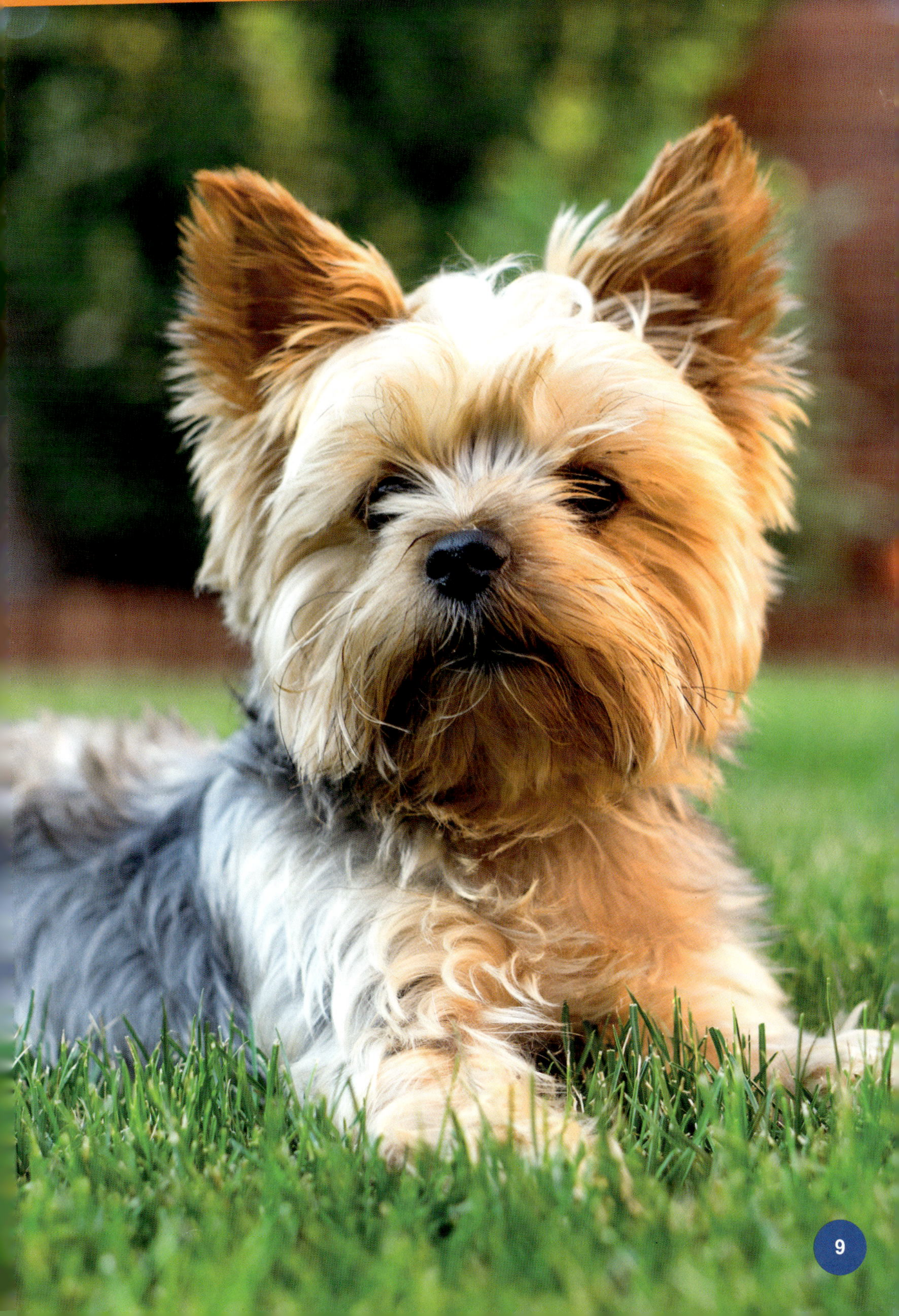

Dog breeds are divided into groups. Yorkshire Terriers are part of the Toy Group, which includes small dogs. However, Yorkies' big personalities are more like the dogs in the Terrier Group. Yorkies are smart, brave, and full of energy. They can also be very independent!

FUN FACT

Yorkie puppies are born black and tan. The color of their hair changes as they get older.

WHERE YORKIES COME FROM

NORWAY
SWEDEN
SCOTLAND
North Sea
IRELAND
ENGLAND
GERMANY
Yorkshire, England
Atlantic Ocean
FRANCE
ITALY
SPAIN

11

Chapter 2
Looking at a Yorkie

Yoyo is tiny. Yorkshire Terriers are one of the smallest dog breeds. Yorkies must weigh seven pounds (3.2 kg) or less to be allowed to compete in **dog shows**. But there are pet Yorkies who are bigger than that.

FUN FACT
If it isn't clipped, a Yorkie's hair can grow up to 2 feet (61 cm) long!

Yoyo is the perfect size for Sophie. She can carry him around easily in a bag and he's not too big to sit on her lap.

Sophie loves to stroke his long, straight hair. It's parted along his back and flows all the way down to the bottom of his tummy! She brushes it every day. To keep the hair out of Yoyo's eyes, Sophie ties it into a bow on the top of his head.

CUTTING HAIR

A Yorkie's hair is a bit like yours. It keeps growing unless you cut it. Some Yorkshire Terriers have their hair clipped short into a puppy cut. The short haircut is easier to take care of.

THE YORKIE

MALES AND FEMALES

HEIGHT*:
7–8 in. (18–20 cm)

WEIGHT:
7 lbs. or less (3.2 kg or less)

TAIL
Held higher than the back

COAT
Silky, glossy, can reach to the floor

*The height of a dog is measured from the top of the shoulder, not from the top of the head.

EARS
Point upward

FACE
Sparkling, intelligent expression

HAIR
Parted along spine from skull back to tail

FEET
Round with black toenails

Chapter 3
Meet a Yorkshire Terrier!

Sit! Stay! Roll over! Play dead! Sophie has taught Yoyo all kinds of tricks. Like a typical Yorkie, Yoyo is smart and curious. He loves to learn new things. Sophie started training Yoyo the day her family brought him home. Because Yorkies were originally working dogs, they are good at following instructions. Sophie uses food and praise to reward Yoyo. He loves getting a treat and being told he's a good boy. He loves the attention!

IN ACTION!

Yorkshire Terriers are great at a dog sport called agility. They enjoy learning to jump, crawl through tunnels, and zigzag around poles. Dogs and their owners compete to see which dog can put up the fastest time through an obstacle course.

Sophie tosses a small ball across the yard. Yoyo eagerly scurries after it. Yorkies love to play. Yoyo's favorite game is chase. That makes sense, because Yorkshire Terriers were bred to hunt small animals. If you have a smaller pet, like a rat, a hamster, or a lizard, be careful! Don't leave them alone with a Yorkie.

Sophie spends a lot of time playing with Yoyo. She's always very gentle, though. He's so small that he could easily get hurt.

When Yoyo is done playing, he loves to snuggle with Sophie. He also likes to go out with her in a carry bag. Anything for attention! Yorkies can get upset if they're left alone for too long.

FUN FACT

Yorkshire Terriers were popular lap dogs among English ladies during the late 1800s.

Yorkshire Terriers have a lot of energy. Because they're so small, though, they don't need very long walks. Their tiny feet get a lot of steps in!

Sophie's family doesn't have a backyard, but that's okay. Yorkshire Terriers are great dogs for smaller homes, or even apartments. They do well in cities.

Yorkies are happy if they have something to do and someone to be with.

Yorkshire Terriers like to bark. They won't be as yappy if they're well-trained and have plenty to do.

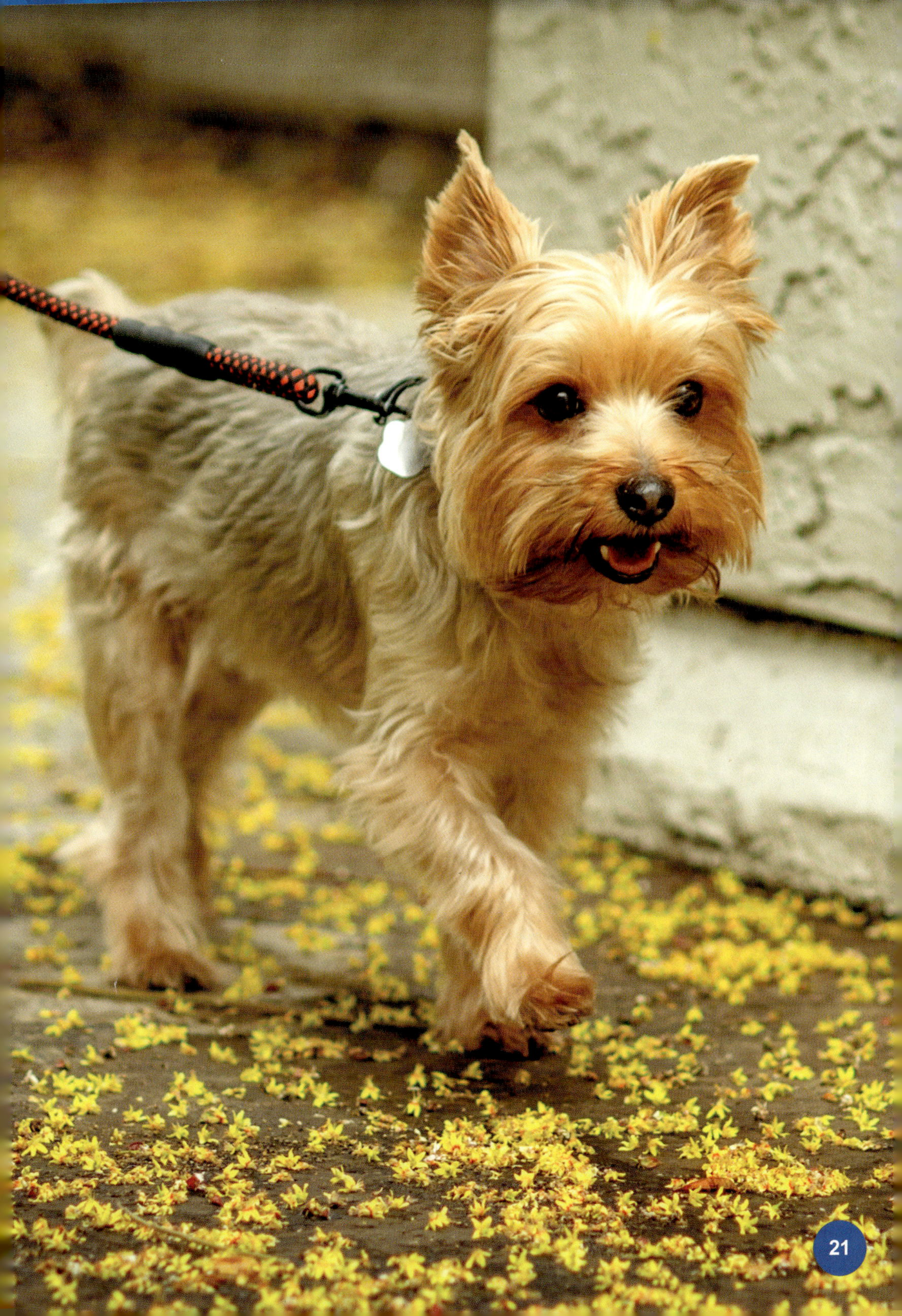

Chapter 4
Caring for a Yorkie

Every afternoon, Sophie puts a **harness** on Yoyo and takes him for a walk. Yoyo's neck is too **delicate** to walk him with a collar. The harness clips around his back and chest.

Sometimes, if it's chilly, Sophie buttons a dog-size coat on Yoyo. Yorkies are small, and their hair is thin. They can easily get cold.

They head out the front door. Yoyo sniffs and struts his way around the neighborhood.

After their walk, Sophie gently brushes Yoyo's long, silky hair. Yorkies need a lot of grooming. Otherwise, their hair can become knotted. Every week, Sophie gives Yoyo a bath. She uses dog shampoo and warm water. Then she dries him off with a towel so he doesn't get cold.

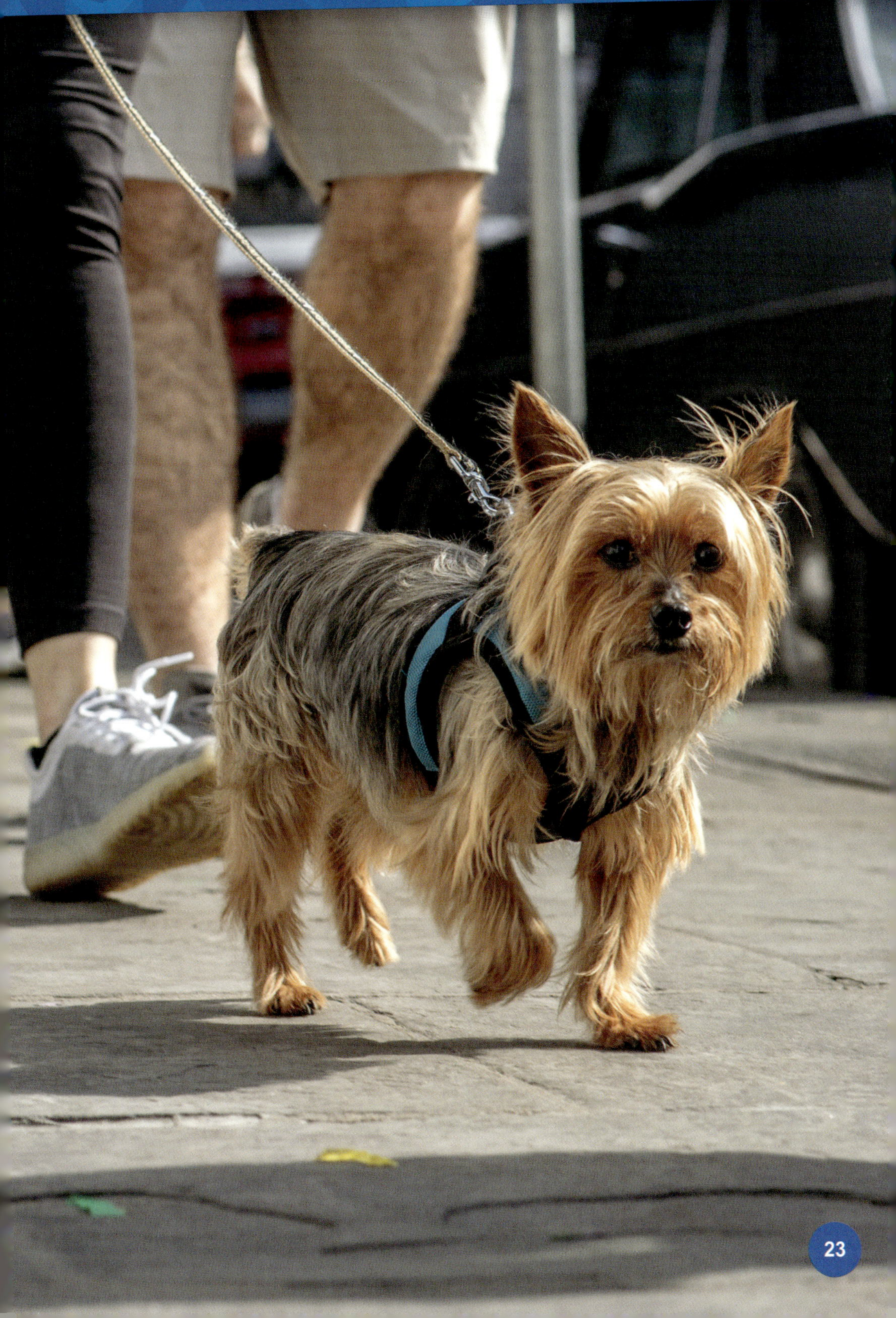

Sophie feeds Yoyo twice a day. He gets healthy food, but not too much of it. And not too many treats! A **veterinarian** warned Sophie to be careful what she feeds him. He said that Yorkies can easily get an upset stomach.

FUN FACT
Bruce Willis, Brett Favre, Justin Timberlake, Orlando Bloom, and Johnny Depp all love Yorkies.

Sophie also makes sure that Yoyo always has fresh water in his bowl.

What about treats? Sophie gives Yoyo treats when he does something good. She makes sure to choose smaller treats that are right for Yorkies.

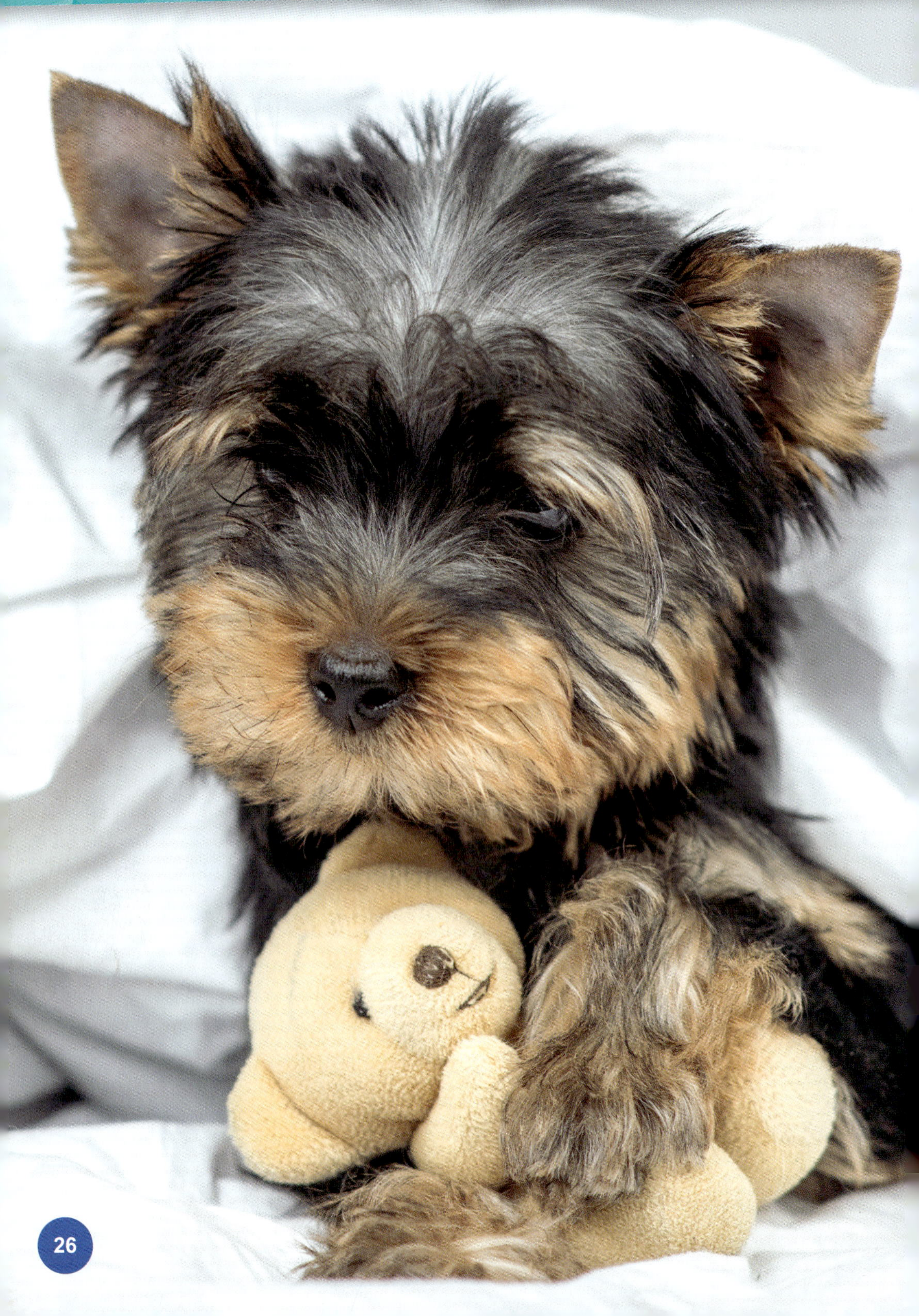

Sophie watches Yoyo curl up, ready to snooze the night away. He tucks his little paws in and lays his head on his feet. He glances up at Sophie, then lets his eyes slowly close.

She wonders what he dreams about. Toys? Treats? Snuggling with his favorite person? "Maybe he dreams about me," Sophie thought. She hoped so!

Like people, dogs need to have clean teeth. Every day, Sophie brushes Yoyo's with special dog toothpaste.

BEYOND
THE BOOK

After reading the book, it's time to think about what you learned. Try the following exercises to jumpstart your ideas.

RESEARCH

FIND OUT MORE. There is so much more to find out about Yorkshire Terriers. Visit the American Kennel Club's site to research Yorkies. Or look for a Yorkshire Terrier Club in your area. You can meet other people who love your favorite breed!

CREATE

TIME FOR ART. Yorkies are just one type of Terrier. Several other dogs are Terriers—Australian, Border, Fox, etc. Look at some pictures of all of these Terriers. Then get some markers and use your imagination. What new breed of Terrier can you create? What will they look like? What will they like to do? What would they be like as pets?

DISCOVER

LOTS OF BREEDS. This book is about your favorite dog breed. But there are hundreds more around the world. Visit the AKC site or those of other dog organizations. What other breeds can you discover? Which breeds are related to your favorite? What is the most interesting new breed you have discovered?

GROW

HELP OUT! Animal shelters can be great places to volunteer. Contact a shelter near you and find out if you can help. Or can your family donate food or gear to help rescue dogs? Find out why dogs end up in shelters. Is there anything you can do to help them find homes?

RESEARCH NINJA

Visit www.ninjaresearcher.com/4477 to learn how to take your research skills and book report writing to the next level!

RESEARCH

DIGITAL LITERACY TOOLS

SEARCH LIKE A PRO
Learn about how to use search engines to find useful websites.

FACT OR FAKE?
Discover how you can tell a trusted website from an untrustworthy resource.

TEXT DETECTIVE
Explore how to zero in on the information you need most.

SHOW YOUR WORK
Research responsibly— learn how to cite sources.

WRITE

GET TO THE POINT
Learn how to express your main ideas.

PLAN OF ATTACK
Learn prewriting exercises and create an outline.

DOWNLOADABLE REPORT FORMS

Further Resources

BOOKS

Adelman, Beth. *Good Dog!: Dog Care for Kids.* Mankato, Minn.: Child's World: 2014.

Beal, Abigail. *I Love My Yorkshire Terrier.* PowerKids Press, 2011.

Schuh, Mari. *Yorkshire Terriers (Blastoff! Readers, Level 2: Awesome Pets).* Bellwether Media, 2014.

WEBSITES

FACTSURFER

Factsurfer.com gives you a safe, fun way to find more information.

1. Go to www.factsurfer.com.
2. Enter "Yorkshire Terriers" into the search box and click.
3. Select your book cover to see a list of related websites.

Glossary

agility: a dog sport where dogs run around an obstacle course.

delicate: easily hurt or damaged.

dog show: a show at which dogs are judged according to breed standards.

harness: straps that fit around the back and chest onto which you can snap a leash.

therapy dog: a dog who is trained to offer affection, comfort, and support.

veterinarian: a doctor for animals.

Index

agility sports, 17
barking, 20
bathing, 22
brushing, 13, 22
dog show, 12
ears, 8, 15
eating, 24
Great Britain, 6
hair, 4, 8, 10, 12, 13, 15, 22
hunting, 6, 18

mines, 6
sleeping, 27
Smoky, 8
teeth, 25, 27
Toy Group, 10
training, 17, 20
veterinarian, 24
walking, 8, 20, 22
World War II, 8
Yorkshire (area), 6

PHOTO CREDITS

The images in this book are reproduced through the courtesy of: iStock.com: Jaroslav Frank 12; omersukrugoksu 17; Andrew Michael 18; kali9 24; Ezumeimages 26. Shutterstock: MNStudio 4; Eve Photography 6; Attila Fodomesi 8; Jagodka 10; Veniamin Kraskov 13; Ermolaev Alexandr 14; Zelenskaya 16; Iakov Filimov 19; Veran36; Stowen Sato 20; Metha19 21; tkemot 22; Mikhail Bezdenezhnykh 23; Scorpp 25; Kachalkina Veronika 27; Scorpp 31.
Cover and page 1: Csanad Kiss/Shutterstock. Paw prints: Maximillian Laschon/Shutterstock.

About the Author

Anna Davison writes about science, nature and health. She loves animals and has cared for dogs, cats, fish, frogs, and flatworms!